D1004860

gift books by kimberly rinehart and georgia rettmer:
tapestry of joy ...a gift of friendship
colors of hope ...a gift of encouragement

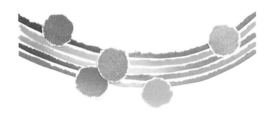

published and distributed exclusively by
The C.R. Gibson Company, a division of Thomas Nelson, Inc.
by special arrangement with
♥ it takes two® ♥
le sueur, minnesota.

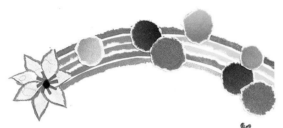

to: BRYAN and NADJA

from: STEFANY

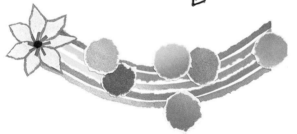

published by C.R. Gibson,® Norwalk, Connecticut 06856

C.R. Gibson® is a registered trademark of Thomas Nelson, Inc.

printed in the United States of America

GB672 ISBN 0-7667-5391-3

tapestry of joy
. . . a gift of friendship

written by kimberly rinehart
illustrated by georgia rettmer

The C.R. Gibson Company, Norwalk, Connecticut 06856

because of you,
i walk upon a rainbow trail
and feel a song of laughter
in my heart.

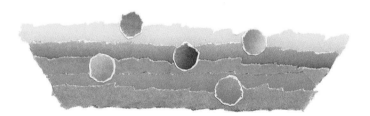

because of you,
i know the comfort of a companion
and the love
of a friend.

because of you,

i've learned to speak
with my heart
and find peace in the healing power
of silence.

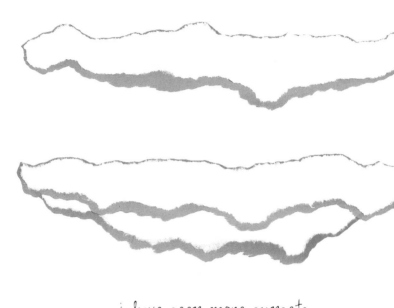

i have seen more sunsets,
made more memories
and felt more alive

than i ever dared to believe possible.

i count
our friendship
as a gift to be treasured
and a blessing to be shared . . .

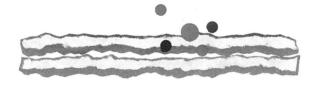

and i can reach out knowing that
a caring heart
will somehow always find me.

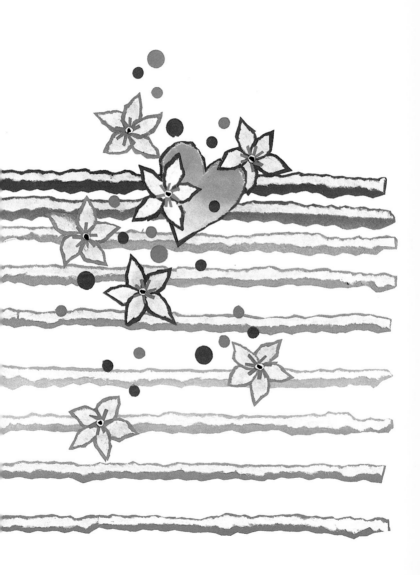

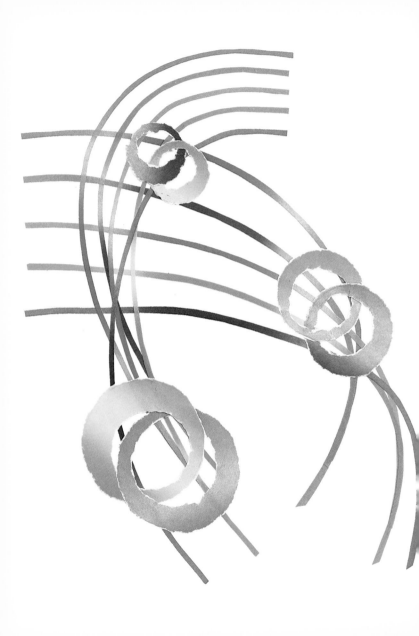

with you, i see how God can weave
two different lives together
and create a tapestry of joy

and just because of you

the sun feels warmer
and small worries seem to fade . . .

for you have a way
of showing me
the things that really matter

and even when we're far apart

i never feel alone.

i can see myself grow stronger
in the presence of our friendship,
and i'll be forever grateful
just to have you in my life.

your laughter warms my spirit
like an old familiar song
and your thoughtfulness
surprises me with joy.

our friendship always gives us room
for honesty to grow
and our fears can find
a place to safely rest.

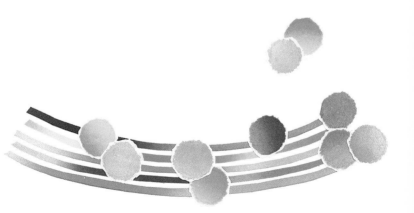

the times we spend together
are like footprints in the sand
washing gently into memories
all too soon . . .

. . . and like the gentle winds of autumn,

like the tenderness of spring

the seasons of our friendship
will surround us.

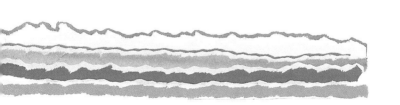

when i think of all the people
who have helped my heart to grow
my grateful thoughts
will always be of you

for our lives have grown together,
our paths have intertwined
and left the colors of our hearts
forever changed

and my silent prayer
will always be

that somewhere in their lives . . .

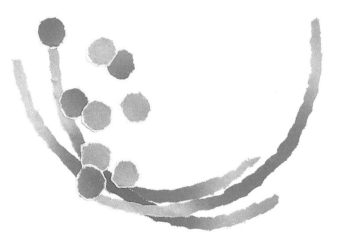

. . . everyone will have a friend
like you.

i know true friendship
is a gift that lasts forever
and the quiet hands of time
will make us strong.

because of you,

i dare to share my dreams
and follow them . . .

believing . . .

and my heart
will always have a special place
to feel
at
home.